Original title:
The Watchmaker's Dream

Copyright © 2025 Creative Arts Management OÜ
All rights reserved.

Author: Jameson Hartfield
ISBN HARDBACK: 978-1-80586-131-7
ISBN PAPERBACK: 978-1-80586-603-9

Dial of Destiny

In a workshop filled with ticking tunes,
Screws and springs dance like clumsy loons.
A gear lost its way, took a spin,
Ended up tangled in a cat's whim.

Clock hands chase each other in jest,
'Time's a joke,' the old watch said with zest.
But when seconds giggle and hours prance,
Who needs a watch? Let's just dance!

Momentary Landscapes

A second confirmed it was really late,
But the hour hand just couldn't relate.
Painting sunsets in odd shades of green,
The clock sighed, 'Shouldn't I intervene?'

Each tick is a sketch, each tock a spree,
Drawing landscapes where time can't flee.
With every twist, a new scene appears,
The artist? A watch with a few loose gears!

The Pulse Beyond Time

A watch with a heart beats soft and slow,
It giggles and grins, putting on a show.
With every pulse, it ponders deep,
'When's nap time? I could use some sleep.'

The pendulum swings, like a swing at play,
'Time is a river,' the old watch would say.
But if rivers could laugh, they'd run dry,
Too busy sharing jokes that fly high!

Whims of the Clock

A clock with a mustache, so dandy and bright,
Stirred up chaos from morning till night.
It whispered to seconds, 'Let's play hide and seek,'
Leaving minutes bewildered, feeling quite weak.

As hours wore sombreros, dancing in cheer,
The watch burst out laughing, fueled by good beer.
When time plays pranks with a cheeky grin,
You know that the fun has only begun!

The Hands of Creation

In a shop where time does jiggle,
A clock's hand dances, causing a giggle.
Springs are bouncing, whirs abound,
Each tick and tock, a joyful sound.

Gears wear hats, and pendulums sway,
Laughing at minutes that want to play.
The hourglass chuckles, grains in a race,
As it spills sand with a playful grace.

Watches grinned as they chime chime chime,
Every tock is a funny rhyme.
Repairmen trip over tools in delight,
While time keeps moving, oh what a sight!

In this realm of tinker and twist,
Not a second goes amiss or missed.
With laughter loud and joy supreme,
They craft the quirkiest of every dream.

Moments in Motion

Every moment hops like a kangaroo,
Ticking clocks hold a funny view.
Minutes march with silly shoes,
In a parade where no one snooze.

Bouncing seconds in a line-up,
Juggling time like a mock-up.
Silly faces on dials grin wide,
Each tick a prank, nothing to hide.

Hours do cartwheels, nothing amiss,
Winking gears send clocks a kiss.
In this circus where time does twirl,
Every second's a bellyache whirl.

So grab your watch and dance with glee,
Join this fun time jubilee.
Moments gathered, laughter's the potion,
In this wacky world of joyful motion.

A Symphony of Cogs

Cogs are singing a merry tune,
Twirling 'round like a cartoon.
The symphony of gears plays sweet,
A funny ballet on tiny feet.

With each rotation, a giggle bursts,
Every clock dance quenches thirsts.
Ball bearings spin with a winking eye,
As seconds zoom through the sky.

Instruments of time play pranks anew,
A metronome shuffles, oh what a view!
Tick-tock orchestras hit every note,
Creating music in a wobbly boat.

So listen closely, hear the cheer,
As the cogs croon, drawing near.
In this gala of laughter and glee,
Time's funny waltz sets spirits free.

Dreams in the Balance

On a scale where seconds are tossed,
Dreams teeter lightly, never lost.
Balancing time with a feather's grace,
Laughing as moments race the space.

Ticking treasures lined in a row,
Balancing joy alongside the flow.
One minute wobbles, another leans,
In playful chaos, laughter gleans.

Caught in a jester's playful trance,
Time does the cha-cha, given a chance.
Silly dreams float on a see-saw high,
With each heartbeat, they twirl and fly.

So raise your glass to the antics near,
Each tick a jest, each tock a cheer.
In this madcap blend of sway and chance,
Dreams balance, inviting us to dance.

Rhythm of the Pendulum

In a land where time does sway,
A pendulum dances, a waltz in play.
It ticks and tocks, a laugh it brings,
As seconds slip by on tiny wings.

With each swing, it hums a tune,
While clocks giggle beneath the moon.
A chorus of watches join in glee,
In this whimsical time symphony.

Crafting Time's Story

With a wink, the gears align,
Each tick a tale, oh so fine.
Crafted memories, they spin and twirl,
As minutes dance in a joyful whirl.

A crooked smile on the hour's face,
Time's mischief finds a perfect place.
A craft of laughter, a joke on display,
In the realm where seconds play.

The Art of Precision

With a tiny tool in a deft little hand,
A clockmaker dreams of a tick-tock band.
He tunes each gear with a tiny chime,
Making all moments seem truly sublime.

A mischievous twist and a cheeky grin,
He counts the laughs in the time tucked in.
In perfect measure, with quirky rhymes,
He masters the art of jester's chimes.

Silent Gears

In the belly of clocks, laughter is found,
While silent gears do their merry round.
They sway in secret, they grin, they cheer,
In a world where tick-tocks disappear.

A hidden joke between the springs,
As time unravels its funny things.
Whispers of laughter in every tick,
In this clockwork, humor plays a trick.

Between the Hands

In a world where gears do play,
A tick tock dance leads the way.
Watches wink with cheeky grins,
Time slips by, yet laughter spins.

Mice chase shadows on the floor,
While clocks debate just who's a bore.
Silly springs – they jump and prance,
Each second's wink, a quick romance.

Time's Gentle Hands

Ticklish hands on a clock face,
Doodles swirling, not a race.
Each second's giggle fills the air,
Time jests, with a playful flair.

Sundials chuckle in the sun,
As clocks insist they've had their fun.
Twirling moments make us sway,
Watch out! They'll have the last say!

A Clockwork Heart

A heart of cogs, it starts to beat,
With every tick, it finds a beat.
Laughter springs from winding gears,
As time hums soft, cancelling fears.

In workshops filled with jest and cheer,
Each bolt and screw would like a beer.
With silly tunes, they croon all day,
"Just wind us up, and we'll play!"

Whispers in the Cogs

Cogs whisper secrets in the night,
Spinning tales of sheer delight.
Giggling gears make mischief loud,
While tick-tock tockers form a crowd.

Hands that jest and dials that wink,
With every chime, they slyly link.
A merry tune of gears at play,
In this clockwork world – come sway!

The Alchemy of Time

Tick tock, the clock does jig,
It dances round like a cheerful pig.
Each gear sings a silly tune,
While minutes vanish like a balloon.

Cogs and springs in laughter spin,
Chasing the hours with a cheeky grin.
A pendulum swings, full of glee,
Time's a jester, wild and free.

In this workshop made of gold,
Laughing mechanics never grow old.
Every tick brings a comic plight,
As we bumble through day and night.

So here we stand, hands all a-jerk,
In this odd little clockmaker's quirk.
Time's not a task, but a joke we share,
A merry dance in the vibrant air.

Restless Mechanisms

Gears collide with a clang and chime,
Creating chaos, oh what a crime!
Ticking clocks all break into dance,
In this wild place where watches prance.

Wrenches giggle, springs spring out,
What's a clock without a little shout?
Screwdrivers spin like they own the floor,
In this madcap shop behind the door.

Time gets tangled like unruly hair,
As the mechanisms frolic without a care.
They chuckle and ponder in metal debates,
While moments trip over their own states.

Laughing at hours that never seem steady,
Each second bounces like a jelly confetti.
For in this realm of endless tick,
Restless dreams can be quite the trick.

Visions in the Gears

Gears whisper secrets, oh what a sight,
Turning round with a twinkle so bright.
Watches giggle, clocks share a wink,
In this metal dance, what do you think?

A timepiece joked about missing a beat,
While springs hopped like they're on their feet.
Ticking away with comedic flair,
Every whirring wonder shows they care.

Dreams made of brass and enigma's glow,
Carry a laughter wherever they go.
In the realm of time where laughter is bold,
Funny fables in gears unfold.

Clock hands race like children at play,
Chasing the sun till it fades away.
With each tick-tock, a jest to behold,
Visions abound that never grow old.

Temporal Tapestry

A tapestry woven with threads of time,
All stitched together in a jolly rhyme.
Clocks prance and giggle, what a delight,
Every second brings laughter, day and night.

Winding mechanisms tell silly tales,
With every tick, merriment prevails.
In a world where moments are filled with jest,
Time hurries by, never taking a rest.

Cogs that cackle, hands that swirl,
In this funny clock, life's a twirl.
Jests of the past join the future's play,
As laughter echoes in a whimsical way.

So let us gather in this grand design,
Where time is silly and clocks align.
In this lovely mix of fun and cheer,
The tapestry of time brings joy near.

Reflections in Brass

In a shop filled with tick-tock tunes,
Brass gears dance like silly buffoons.
A watch with a grin, a wobbly face,
Says, 'Hurry up now, keep up the pace!'

Sprockets giggle and springs have fun,
Tickling seconds 'til the day is done.
With every chime, they tell a jest,
Time's a trickster; it knows no rest!

Winding tales in a playful spin,
Each tick's a chuckle, where to begin?
The cuckoo stutters, a comical sight,
As laughter echoes from day to night!

So in this realm, where laughter springs,
The hands of time dance on silly strings.
With every hour, a fresh delight,
In this merry world, all is bright!

Threads of Time

In a loom where seconds weave,
Threads of laughter begin to cleave.
A stitch of joy in every row,
Time's fabric ripples with humor's glow.

With needles that giggle, they sew the hours,
Creating moments that bloom like flowers.
A patch of fun in the quilt of day,
Sews smiles in the patterns, come what may!

Twisting and turning, each loop a jest,
Woven memories we simply detest.
Yet laughter holds them, soft and tight,
In threads of time, everything feels right!

So come join the dance, and stitch your dreams,
A tapestry bright with laughter's gleams.
For in this fabric, you'll always find,
The joy of existence, humor entwined!

Cascade of Moments

Like water that tumbles with giggly glee,
Moments cascade, come splash with me!
Each drop a chuckle, each splash a cheer,
In this river of time, there's little to fear.

Raindrops resembling a ticklish prank,
Drip from the sky like a funny tank.
Bubbles dance by, full of gleeful charm,
Carrying laughter, a joyous alarm!

In this stream, the fishes jest,
With scales of humor, they're dressed the best.
Coral reefs giggle with every wave,
In this liquid world, every heart is brave!

So dive into moments, let laughter flow,
In the cascade of fun, let your joy grow.
For time is a river, in motion and rhyme,
With every splash, savor the climb!

The Calendar's Canvas

On a canvas bright, the days unfold,
Each month a picture, a story told.
With colors of chuckles and laughter so bold,
Time paints its canvas, a sight to behold!

Forget the blues of a rainy day,
For each square's filled with a comical play.
Balloons and cakes on special dates,
When the tickling humor delights and waits.

With doodles and scribbles, the months parade,
Every weekend warns, "Let's not be late!"
A swirl of merriment marks the weeks,
As every tick-tock whispers funny tweaks!

So flip the pages, let laughter bloom,
In this calendar world, there's always room.
For each little moment, a giggle can spark,
On this canvas of time, we all leave our mark!

Mending Time's Tapestry

In a shop where clock hands wiggle,
Time ticks on with a silly giggle.
Gears twist like jelly in a jar,
As seconds dance beneath a star.

Wrenches clash in a comical fight,
While springs revolt, much to delight.
Cogs complain, with a whiny tone,
As laughter echoes in the zone.

The pendulum swings like a pendulum's foe,
Ticking in patterns we barely know.
With each tick that skips like a hop,
Time chuckles as it won't stop.

So here in this space where time's a prank,
A watchmaker grins, and his treasures crank.
Mending the fabric with joyous cheer,
Making each moment feel bright and clear.

Rustling Hours

Tick-tock! What a riot, my friend,
Hours whirl like leaves in the wind.
Sundials giggle, casting long shade,
While clocks pull pranks, oh what a charade!

Minutes bump like children at play,
Giggling echoes in their own way.
The sun winks, with mischief in mind,
As shadows grow longer, tangled but kind.

Each hour a jester, with laughter so loud,
Chasing the moments, boisterous and proud.
Ticking along, on laughter's sweet trail,
Time twists and twirls like a whimsical tale.

So join the frolic, don't be a bore,
These rustling hours, who could ask for more?
With every tick, let the fun unwind,
In this merry dance, what gems we find!

The Clockmaker's Canvas

On a canvas of gears and shining brass,
Ticking masterpieces create a fine class.
Colors of time paint the world so bright,
Watchmaker's whimsy is pure delight.

He splashes seconds like paint in the air,
Each brush stroke twisted, beyond compare.
Hours leap across the vibrant display,
While rusting clocks giggle at their decay.

With each tick, a chuckle escapes,
As time twirls in capes and various shapes.
The pendulums pirouette and sway,
Bringing joy to the mundane ballet.

So let's celebrate this artful view,
Where watches chuckle and moments renew.
In the gallery of giggles, let time be free,
For art, and laughter, is the best decree.

Fragments of Infinity

In pieces of hours that twinkle and pied,
Time giggles wildly, like a child tried.
With fragments of moments, they scatter about,
Creating a medley, like laughter's shout.

Infinity hops on a trampoline high,
Bouncing off laughter, oh me, oh my!
Tick-tock, tick-tock, like frogs in a pond,
Waves of mirth in the clockwork respond.

Each second a puzzle, a joke to unfold,
Twisting and turning, never too old.
In the corridors of giggling space,
Time's fragments dance in a merry race.

So gather the pieces, let joy be our guide,
In this grand collection, we'll take in our stride.
In playful fragments, we find our delight,
Making time's journey a whimsical flight.

Beneath the Brass Stars

In a shop where gears spin and whir,
A clock chimed five, then said, "Burr!"
A mouse with a cap snuck up on the floor,
It laughed at the tick, then danced out the door.

The pendulum swings like a pendulous swing,
It tickled the tinker; oh, what a fling!
A wrench played the trumpet, a watch wore a hat,
As bolts started jigging, and springs went splat!

Jovial grins graced each metal face,
As they jive and boogie in a starry place.
The cuckoo decided to shake and to shimmy,
Time's not taken too seriously, oh, isn't it zippy?

Under shining brass stars, gears turn around,
Even time can dance; it's a sight to be found.
With laughter and rhythm, they sway to a tune,
Who knew that a watch could bust a move like a loon!

Hands of Fate

Oh, those hands that tick, they have such flair,
One spins around like it just don't care.
The minute hand slips, like a mischievous clown,
It flipped the hour, then tripped, fell down.

Each tick a joke, with time on their side,
The hour laughs, oh, what a ride!
A toe-tapping tickle, a twist of the wrist,
They giggle together; oh, how could we resist?

A clock with a charm that never grows old,
Its stories of laughter are just joy to behold,
In their world of numbers and quirky laughs,
They tickle the silence, oh, what daft crafts!

Hands of fate, with mischief they play,
Turning the mundane into a grand ballet.
With each little tick, a giggle in time,
Caught in their rhythm, oh, isn't it prime?

The Art of Time's Embrace

In a workshop where laughter mixes with gears,
Time takes a break; it wipes away tears.
A watch winks slyly, knowing it's a jest,
While scissors were laughing, they all jested best.

The art of tick-tock, a game of silly,
With cogs that smile and a crank that's frilly.
A clock's face was grinning, a mischief-filled sight,
As wrenches played hopscotch by the soft candlelight.

Dancing in circles, each gear knew the plan,
A funny little waltz, led by a fan.
The hours flew by on the wings of a joke,
Time covers its mouth, trying hard not to choke.

Embraced by the humor, no moments to waste,
They tickled the seconds; what fun it's to haste!
In this whimsical world, where laughter counts most,
Each tick is a giggle, a clocksmith's great boast.

Mechanisms of Memory

In a box of trinkets, memories collide,
Each cog holds a chuckle; time laughs with pride.
A fuse blew a raspberry, oh what a sight,
As memories danced in soft, twinkly light.

Gears recall stories, both silly and bright,
A mix-up of times amplifies the delight.
The clock giggled softly as it faced the past,
It told uncountable tales—some silly, some fast.

With moments of laughter, they wind up the fun,
A tickle of joy in the rays of the sun.
Every turn of a screw crafts a tale you won't miss,
Each clink and each clank brings a smile or a kiss.

Mechanisms of memory, so quirky yet fine,
Each tick is a treasure, each tock is divine.
So bring on the laughter, the goofiness too,
With rhythm and tickles, there's magic in you!

Dreams in the Mechanism

In a world of springs and gears,
Ticking clocks hide all their fears.
A squirrel dances with a key,
While mice conduct the symphony.

Each tick-tock brings a giggle,
As hands of time start to wiggle.
The pendulum sings a silly tune,
Under the gaze of a sleepy moon.

Cogs and wheels play hide and seek,
Chasing laughter, never meek.
In every setback, moments gleam,
The jester in a watchmaker's dream.

So come, let's wind this merry clock,
Time to giggle, tick and rock!
A playful twist in the dial's embrace,
We'll leave behind a funny trace.

The Ticker's Serenade

A clock chimed softly, full of cheer,
Its tick-tock melody, we all can hear.
Dancing gears in a joyous parade,
A spectacle in brass and jade.

The hour hand swirls with flair,
While second hand dives in midair.
Time sometimes thinks it's quite the jest,
As whirling nuts pull off a fest.

Winding springs hum a cheeky tune,
As time does the cha-cha 'neath the moon.
And if a watch gets a little stuck,
It chuckles, "Well, good luck!"

So listen close, dear friend of mine,
To the music that ticks in every line.
With every tock, let laughter dwell,
In the singer's, tick-tock, heartfelt spell.

Cosmic Clockwork

Stars twinkle in the cosmos bright,
Ticking softly through the night.
Galaxies spin, a dizzy waltz,
As comets chuckle in their vaults.

Time's a jester dressed as space,
With all its knots, a playful grace.
Black holes giggle, spinning around,
While planets jive without a sound.

Each tick a wink from far away,
As time conspirators dance and play.
The universe sways, a cosmic blast,
With humor woven in its vast.

So let's toast to this big clock face,
With starlight, quarks, and endless grace.
For every moment is a chance to gleam,
In this whimsical, cosmic scheme.

Sculptor of Time

A sculptor carves with subtle roles,
Chipping laughs from ticking souls.
With every stroke, the joy unfolds,
As past and future twirl like molds.

Watches giggle, each a sprite,
Sculpted smiles, oh what a sight!
Ticklish faces on every side,
Crafting fun where treasures hide.

With chisels made from sparkling light,
The artist grins, oh what a sight!
As hours dance like playful sprites,
And time forgets its heavy fights.

So wind up joy, let spirits clank,
In this workshop where laughter swank.
In every tick, a giggle's found,
In the sculptor's world, where joy abounds.

Eternal Cadence

In a world where time just grins,
A watch in need of some new fins.
It ticks and tocks with such delight,
The gears dance wildly, day and night.

With springs that leap and dials that spin,
A clock debates, 'Where have you been?'
It strikes up tunes of jellybeans,
And hums about those quirky scenes.

Each minute's like a playful tease,
As seconds stroll with playful ease.
The hour hand winks at passerby,
While every tick just shouts "Oh my!"

So raise a glass to time's mad fate,
With gears that jiggle, diets of fate.
For in this watchman's zany world,
Time's silly flag has been unfurled.

The Fabric of Moments

Stitching moments with threads of rhyme,
In a patchwork quilt that laughs at time.
Each tick a thread, each tock a seam,
In a fabric woven from a dream.

Buttons that smile and zippers that cheer,
Fabric soft as cotton, no need to fear.
With every fold a silly tale,
Of pockets sown with playful wail.

A spool of laughter rolls away,
Mismatched socks go out to play.
The needle bent with too much fun,
Sewing stories 'til the day is done.

So dance with fabric, dance with light,
Embrace the funny, day or night.
Time's a tailor with a crazy plot,
Stitching moments, like it or not.

Horological Hues

Colors clash in perfect tune,
Painted cogs that make us swoon.
Time's a palette, bold and bright,
In a world of day and night.

A clock painted like a clown,
Wears a funny, oversized gown.
With every tick, it shows its hues,
Making art while we just snooze.

Tick-tock tune, a vibrant beat,
Dancing rhythms underneath our feet.
Time's a brush with strokes so wild,
Each moment's like a playful child.

So splash the canvas, fill it high,
Let laughter echo, let joy fly.
For in this world of colors bright,
Time's a jester, full of light.

In the Mind of a Tinkerer

In a cluttered space where wonders dwell,
A mind that ticks like a curious bell.
Wrenches giggle, and screws delight,
As ideas launch into the night.

Oil cans spill their secrets fair,
While springs conspire to shake the air.
With doodads dancing in a row,
The tinkerer laughs, 'What a show!'

Every gadget tells a joke,
In a universe of smoke and yolk.
A nut calls out to a bold screw,
'Let's make a rocket from my shoe!'

So don your apron, hold your prize,
As clocks decide to improvise.
In the tinkerer's world, we find our cheer,
Where whimsy thrives, and fun is near.

Under the Gaze of Time

Tick-tock goes the silly clock,
Winding up to dance and mock.
Its hands are feet, oh what a sight,
Swinging round with pure delight.

Gears like jelly, wobble and sway,
Counting laughs in a joking play.
Each hour tickles with a cheer,
Time's a prankster, let's give a cheer!

Nutty clocks with faces wide,
Chasing seconds, a joyful ride.
With bouncing springs and silly beats,
Every moment, a circus feat!

Under the gaze of time's big grin,
Life's a jest where we all spin.
So grab your hat, let laughter chime,
Join the dance of the playful time.

The Fabric of Seconds

In a loom of tickling threads,
We weave our days, fooling heads.
Silly patterns, mischief sewn,
Each moment's made to wander alone.

Buttons pop and stitches flee,
Every second, a jubilee.
Measuring giggles, counting blinks,
Who knew time could play and think?

Woven dreams on a quilt of hours,
Sprouting joy like blooming flowers.
Tangled laughter in every seam,
Life's a tapestry, a funny dream.

With fabric light and colors bright,
Each tick a burst of pure delight.
Time's a weaver, what a show,
A jester's cloth we all can know!

The Artisan's Lullaby

Hush now, the spindles spin,
Crafting winks from within.
Each hum a giggle, soft and sweet,
Time whispers, "Get up on your feet!"

In workshops bright with playful mess,
Clocks craft tales of silliness.
Wooden dolls with ticking hearts,
Dance around with silly arts.

Sawdust giggles fill the air,
As we spin our dreams with flair.
An artisan's lullaby of cheer,
Singing to the ticks we hear.

With each little twist and shove,
Creating moments full of love.
Sleeping clocks watch over dreams,
Tickling time with joyful beams.

Shadows of Precision

In shadows cast by gears that play,
Time tiptoes in a comical way.
Counting chuckles, it tries to hide,
Behind the moments that slide and glide.

Dancing shadows on the wall,
Making faces, having a ball.
Precision laughs, a sneaky game,
Every tick, a joke to claim.

Tools that wink and cogs that tease,
Making precision feel like breeze.
Crafting smiles in every tick,
Life's funny clockwork, quick and slick!

In the shadows, laughter grows,
Time's a jester, as everyone knows.
So let's embrace the playful rhyme,
In the silly dance of merry time.

The Imagination of Gears

In a shop where clocks tick fast,
Gears seem to be having a blast.
One thought it could dance a jig,
While the others laughed, a bit too big.

Sprockets spun on the countertop,
Dreaming of a funny hop.
A winder with a silly grin,
Planned a party for all within.

With each tick, they teased the hour,
Claiming each second's a superpower.
When the bell strikes, do they care?
Not a chance; they're in mid-air!

Time laughed and wobbled too,
As gears turned in a wacky stew.
Who knew mechanics could be so spry?
With clockwork giggles, they reach for the sky!

Tides of Time

In the ocean of days so bright,
Waves of minutes cause delight.
Surfboards made of hand-spring springs,
Catch the laughter that time brings.

Each wave a tick, each splash a tock,
Riding rhythms on the clock.
Seagulls squawk in playful jest,
Counting seconds, never rest.

A dolphin leaps, a timepiece flop,
Together they spin and pop.
Forget the rush, let's take a ride,
On tides of joy, not time's strict tide.

When hours swirl in a happy trance,
Even clocks must try to dance.
So let's laugh with the ocean's rhyme,
And surf the waves of silly time!

Constellations Above

Stars twinkle with a winking plan,
Growing rumors in a cosmic span.
Galaxies giggle and twirl around,
As supernovas laugh at what they found.

The Milky Way spins a creamy tale,
Of comets who tried to hitch a sail.
Asteroids chuckle, asteroids cheer,
In the vast sky, there's fun over here!

Planets waltz a merry dance,
Taking every chance to prance.
Saturn's rings, oh what a sight,
Joking with Mars all through the night.

When eyesight fades in the black of space,
Stars still play their splendid chase.
Let's gaze up, feel their glee,
For the cosmos is a comedy!

The Chime of Possibilities

Bells ring with a playful jive,
Turning echoes into a lively hive.
Each chime a chance to sing or dance,
In the rhythm of a cosmic trance.

A cuckoo pops with a cheeky smile,
Clock hands spinning, quite the style.
Join in the fun, don't miss the beat,
Time is a party, so grab a seat!

Bells share secrets of dreams long sought,
With every chime, we laugh, we plot.
Tick-tock tales of what might be,
A world of whimsy, come, let's see!

So embrace the sound of endless play,
With every chime, let worries stray.
In this clockwork carnival so clear,
Time's just a joke, so laugh, my dear!

Nebulas of Time

In a shop with gears and springs,
A clockhead sings and swings.
Each tick a laugh, each tock a cheer,
Time plays tricks, oh let's be clear.

With pendulums that dance and twirl,
A whirlwind of seconds in a whirl.
Cogs that giggle, hour hands prance,
In a merry waltz, they take their chance.

The minute hand winks, a sly little glance,
While clocks engage in a cheeky dance.
Laughter echoes in the tick-tock beat,
Where every hour's a comical feat.

Oh, in this clockwork, find your glee,
For time is but a jester, you see.
So grab a laugh from the heart of the chime,
In this whimsical world of nebulas of time.

Etchings on Eternity

After midnight, gears creak and squeal,
A canvas of time, oh what a deal!
With scribbles of moments, joyfully flawed,
Each tick a comic strip, slightly awed.

The grand escapement grins wide with pride,
As memories flash, our laughter collides.
In the clock's heart, a story unfolds,
With punchlines waiting, and excitement untold.

Each hour a doodle, drawn with finesse,
A sketchbook of time, in its goofy dress.
With whimsical scribes, they bounce and gleam,
Etchings of life, oh what a dream!

So let us unravel these ticklish lines,
In the fabric of time, where humor entwines.
Tick the pages with joy, let's take our flight,
In the art of eternity, all feels just right.

Reverberations of Twilight

In the twilight hour, clocks take a bow,
With whimsical echoes, they wonder how.
As shadows stretch and giggles unfold,
Time chuckles softly, a tale to be told.

The moonlight on gears sends whispers of fun,
As seconds race by like they've just begun.
Each chime a snicker, each bell a guffaw,
In the laughter of hours, we find what we saw.

Tick-tock in rhythm, with a bounce in its beat,
Each moment a jest, oh isn't it sweet?
As the stars play twinkles, time has a blast,
In the reverberations, our giggles are cast.

So as dusk settles in with a wink from the past,
We dance through the seconds, joy unsurpassed.
Let's savor the chuckles that evening brings,
In this playful twilight, where merriment sings.

Ticking Fantasies

In a world where dreams take time's hand,
Clocks spin stories, oh isn't it grand?
With hands that tickle and wink with delight,
They create a ballet, a comical sight.

The dreams are tick-tocks, all jumbled and bright,
In the land of the silly, we frolic at night.
With cuckoos that laugh, and timers that play,
Each second's a jester, leading astray.

A symphony of giggles, a cacophony of cheer,
In the ticking of fantasies, joy draws near.
So let's leap through time in this whimsical dance,
Where each tick is a chance for another bright glance.

So grab your fanciful hats, don't you fret,
For in ticking fantasies, there's no need to bet.
We'll cherish every chuckle and run wild with glee,
In a world where humor is as free as can be.

Gears of Enchantment

In a shop where trinkets spin,
Laughter dances on a whim.
Gears jive in a merry row,
Tick-tock tales begin to flow.

Brass bugs hum with joyous glee,
As clocks wink knowingly at thee.
Juggling time with joyful grace,
Each tick a grin on their face.

Winding laughter fills the air,
While springs stretch in a funny flair.
Dials tickle, hands do prance,
In this clockwork, we all dance.

To the beat of merry time,
Every second makes a rhyme.
In this place where joy is free,
All the world can laugh with me.

Time's Whispered Secrets

A cuckoo hops out with a cheer,
Whispering secrets for all to hear.
Ticking clocks hold jokes inside,
As time plays peek-a-boo, so snide.

The pendulum sways with a wink,
Every swing's a chance to think.
Oh, what mischief minute hands weave,
Time's got tricks up its sleeve!

Sprockets giggle, gears play tricks,
They're sneaky little clockwork wicks.
Each hour a jest, a comic flair,
Laughing time beyond compare.

So pull the lever, give a turn,
For every second, watch and learn.
What once was serious, now a jest,
In this clock, we find our fest.

A Clockwork Reverie

In a dreamsphere made of springs,
Time dances while laughter sings.
A tiny robot waves hello,
As gears giggle in a row.

Tickle the clock with a playful touch,
Watch as its hands wiggle as such.
Every minute a chance to cheer,
Funny faces appear quite near.

Bouncing clocks on a jolly spree,
Singing tunes of jubilee.
Time is jesters, oh what a sight,
In this realm, we play all night.

Who knew moments could be so bright?
In the dance of day and night.
Let's twirl with time, take a chance,
In a world where laughter prance.

The Symphony of Silence

In the stillness, clocks hum low,
Making music, on they go.
Twirling cogs in silent chase,
Giddy whispers fill the space.

Time giggles with a twist and turn,
In this quiet, lanterns burn.
Echoes of joy softly blend,
Each tick a secret, none defend.

A tickle from the hour hand,
Rings laughter through the silent land.
As the minute markers play the fool,
Time invites us to its school.

Amidst the quiet, chuckles soar,
With every chime, we can't ignore.
In this hush, let's dance and sway,
For laughter hides in time's ballet.

Ticking Fantasies

In a shop full of gears, what a sight to behold,
Clock hands doing the cha-cha, or so I've been told.
A cuckoo that croons, in a voice oh so spry,
Winks with a tick-tock as seconds go by.

A sundial with shades, on a sunlit cold day,
Sips lemonade slowly, in its own clumsy way.
While hourglasses giggle, spilling sand on the floor,
Counting their blessings, they just want some more.

Brass bands of mosquitoes, in time they do dance,
As springs twist and twirl in a wild, silly prance.
The minutes, they get tangled in laughter and play,
Oh, what a fine mess that the hours convey.

So come take a peek, at this whimsical space,
Where time's just a jester, wearing joy on its face.
Each tick is a chuckle, each tock is a tease,
In the world of the watch, every moment's a breeze.

Time's Tinkerer

A fellow in goggles with tools galore,
Tinkers each moment like a playful encore.
He measures the giggles, adjusts every sigh,
Crafting joy from the tick-tock that flutters nearby.

His workshop's a circus of shimmering time,
With pendulums swinging in rhythmic, sweet rhyme.
A teapot that whistles with every elapsed beat,
Gets saucy, it pours out both laughter and heat.

Watches that wobble and clocks that do spin,
Dare you to dance, let the fun time begin.
With pencils for hands and a rubber-band heart,
He stitches the minutes as pieces of art.

So come join the fun, don't forget to unwind,
For time is a jester, and laughter, it binds.
Let's revel in moments both silly and bright,
As the tinkerer twinkles, and laughs through the night.

Gears of Reverie

In a world of bright cogs and zany old springs,
Dreams tickle and tease making time do some flips.
A robot in slippers who dances on air,
Spins circles around you without any care.

Each slosh of the minute puts smiles all wide,
As gears chatter secret jokes they can't hide.
A pendulum winks like it knows a good pun,
Counting the giggles till the day's finally done.

Magical gadgets that giggle and chime,
Mimic the sounds of a jester's fun time.
A clock that takes selfies whenever it can,
With frames full of laughter, its biggest fan.

So let's wind up our hearts and be joyous today,
For life's tame clockwork has much more to say.
In the chaos of gears, find the laughter inside,
In tales spun by clocks, fun moments abide.

Clockwork Whispers

Whispers of time, they giggle and grin,
As clocks tell their secrets, where do we begin?
A short ticking tale from a playful old watch,
Paints pictures of dreams that it loves to botch.

With springs made of laughter and faces of joy,
Every second's a game, a delightful decoy.
The gears plot mischief beneath the strong tide,
In this whimsical world, come take a wild ride.

A chime sings like birds but speaks in tick-tock,
With stories of mischief that tickle the clock.
A pendulum swings, warns of mischief ahead,
As laughter cascades, all worries are shed.

So come here, dear friends, and please take a seat,
Watch time play its games, oh so sweet to greet.
In this whimsical play, may your heart feel the glee,
For when clocks start to giggle, you're happy and free.

Nightfall's Precision

In the shop where gears unwind,
A clock speaks truths, unrefined.
Each tick is like a playful jest,
Time dancing in a tiny vest.

A pendulum sways, a cheerful sway,
It sings of moments gone astray.
Oh, how the minutes love to tease,
In this world of clocks, we giggle with ease.

The cuckoo pops with a silly squawk,
Riddling time like a madcap talk.
Faces in the clock wink and grin,
Inviting us to join their spin.

So let's all laugh at time's embrace,
As the hour strikes, it's a wild race.
In the kingdom of dials and chimes,
We find our joy in perfect rhymes.

Whispers of the Hourglass

In the glass where sand does roll,
A sly wind whispers, 'Time's on a stroll.'
Each grain a giggle, each tick a tease,
What folly floats on moments with ease.

An hourglass tipped, a laugh erupts,
Like squirrels with acorns, the seconds corrupt.
'You're late!' cries a grain, 'But isn't it fun?'
As we trip through time—there's no need to run.

The bottom half grumbles, 'Why wait for fate?'
While the top half chortles, 'Open the gate!'
Sands slipping, slipping, in whimsical flight,
We revel in shadows that dance in the light.

So let's spin the dial, let's squeak and spin,
For whispers of time are where we begin.
In this comedy of hours, let laughter resound,
Each moment a treasure that keeps us spellbound.

The Elixir of Time

In a bottle labeled 'Time', jokes brew,
With every sip, a giggle's due.
A swirl of minutes in fizzy delight,
We sip on laughter, day turns to night.

Banana peels in the hours we taste,
Spilling joy without any haste.
Flip a second, a hiccup ensues,
As time takes a turn, there's no time to lose.

Flasks bubbling over with tickling glee,
Potion of moments, oh, give it to me!
A sprinkle of chuckles, a dash of surprise,
Drink in the whimsy before it all flies.

And as clocks tick-tock without any care,
We sip on the sweetness, unbound in the air.
For laughter's the secret, the treasure we find,
In the elixir of time, we leap and unwind!

Anatomy of an Hour

In the spine of the clock, a giggling heart,
The hands flap wildly, a comedic art.
Hour by hour, a silly parade,
Ticking and tocking in playful charade.

Each minute a quirk, each second a jest,
When time spins around, we're all at our best.
'What's the rush?' shouts a whiskered old clock,
'Let's tango with time and dance round the block!'

The gears grumble softly, 'What time is it now?'
As they tickle the minutes, they're caught in a bow.
With laughter as fuel, they crank and they whirl,
Creating a tempest, a time-twirling swirl.

So here in this hour, let merriment reign,
For in the anatomy of time, there's no pain.
Just fun-filled moments, a quirky delight,
As hours frolic freely, from morning till night.

In the Tapestry of Timelessness

In a workshop of gears and whirring sights,
The clocks tick-tock with giggling lights.
Each spring uncoils with a joyful bounce,
Time plays tricks as seconds pounce.

A cuckoo bird hops from a tiny space,
With feathers of chrome, it starts a race.
Minutes chase hours in a silly spree,
While seconds juggle, oh so merrily.

Watches wear wigs, with dials dressed bright,
Ticking away in comedic delight.
The hourglass tumbles, it's lost all grace,
As sand does cartwheels in a wild place.

Little robots dance with polished feet,
Spinning in circles, a mechanical treat.
In this land where time has gone astray,
Laughter echoes in a playful ballet.

Dreams Woven in Steel

In a clockmaker's nook, where shadows play,
Gears spin stories by night and by day.
Sprockets tell jokes as they twirl about,
While time sits grinning, there's no room for doubt.

A watch on the wall seems to wink and gawk,
Ticking away during a whimsical talk.
Seconds wear hats, and minutes prance high,
As time's little secrets whirl by like a pie.

Steel strings strum melodies of merry delight,
As the pendulums waddle in soft moonlight.
Dreams in the cogs do boisterously boom,
As laughter invades every tick-tocking room.

Amongst the brass bells, the fun never ends,
With jokey reflections of time as it bends.
In this merry world where clocks love to sing,
Every tick is a story, every chime a fling.

Echoes of Eternity

In an attic of echoes, quick and bright,
Clocks have a party every starry night.
Tickling the hours with a hum and a dash,
They giggle and wiggle, then suddenly crash.

Every chime dances with a twist and a flip,
As pendulums sway and take an odd trip.
Time's silly stories beam with delight,
In this place where minutes take flight.

The tock-tock brigade prances around,
While clocks with mustaches abound.
Each tick is a jolly, absurd refrain,
As laughter flows like a joyful chain.

Mechanisms ticking in perfect charades,
Sharing their whims in polished parades.
Eternity's echoes, all wrapped in fun,
In a land of time's mischief, the giggles run.

The Dance of Pendulums

In a hall of pendulums swinging in tunes,
Tick-tocking together, they're dancing like loons.
With a wobble and a jig, they sway side to side,
In a ballroom of laughter, where whimsy won't hide.

Each swing tells a story of cheeky delight,
As they spin round and round under soft candlelight.
Clocks join the fun, wearing comical hats,
As gears keep the rhythm with sprightly chitchats.

The minutes join hands, swirling with glee,
While seconds do flips, as wild as can be.
This grand dance of time is a sight to behold,
With humor and joy that never gets old.

So come, take a whirl where the laughter flows,
Amongst all the pendulums, anything goes.
In this merry galas of clockwork and cheer,
Where time dances wildly, nothing to fear.

Harmonies of Helix

In a shop full of clocks, what a sight,
Gears twirl and dance, oh what a delight!
A spring here, a tick there, a crazy tune,
Time winks at us, a mischievous cartoon.

The pendulum swings with a giggle and sway,
Tickling the minutes, making them play.
Cogs in a chorus, they laugh and they spin,
In this crafty realm, let the fun begin!

Watch faces are grinning, as time takes a leap,
Whispers of laughter, secrets to keep.
Bouncing between seconds, oh what a ball,
In the world of this clock, there's joy for us all.

So let's toast to the watches, with hands that all wave,
In this clockwork cabaret, our spirits they save.
Swinging and swaying, let the merriment flow,
For in these fine gears, we're all in the show!

Echoing Moments

Time's a jester in a crazy cap,
With clocks that chuckle and gears that clap.
Echoes of laughter in each tick and tock,
In this wacky realm, it's a merry clockwalk.

A cuckoo pops out, with a quizzical grin,
Tickling the seconds, where chaos begins.
Laughter rounds the corner, spins with delight,
In a world where each moment's a comical flight.

Tick tock, says the pendulum, swinging in cheer,
Winding up joy as each hour draws near.
Time pods of humor, they rapidly flow,
In the symphony of seconds, let hilarity grow!

So gather your moments, let's laugh 'til we'mend,
For with each tick-tock, there's laughter to send.
In a land where the minutes all chuckle and beam,
Life's just a funny, fantastical dream!

Tick Tock Dreams

Oh, the tick tocks chime with a cheer and a glee,
Silly little gears dance like they're wild and free.
A watchmen's whimsy, a jolly old chap,
Poking at clocks, he fell in a trap!

He measures the time with a comical gaze,
With time hiccuping in a jigging craze.
Seconds do somersaults, minutes breakdance,
To the rhythm of laughter, they twirl and prance.

His pocket watches giggle, like it's a joke,
While the hands of the clocks begin to poke.
Watch out! Here comes a minute on a string,
Order's lost in the chaos that laughter can bring!

So join in the fun, let's pause and enjoy,
This tick tock dreamland, a whimsical ploy.
In this zany time realm, we'll hop and we'll skip,
For laughter is golden, let it freely slip!

Lost in the Gears

Wander 'round corners of time gone askew,
Where the cogs tell tall tales in a humorous hue.
A watch from the past waves a silly good day,
While second hands frolic in whimsical play.

A clockface with eyes gives a wink and a blink,
Each tick is a giggle, each tock makes you think.
Gears stuck in a riddle, what do they mean?
Perhaps it's a puzzle, a time-telling scene!

"I lost my tick!" one cog starts to squeal,
"Now we're just tocks, spinning like a wheel!"
They huddle and whisper, a comical crew,
With mischief and laughter, they know what to do.

So here in the gears, with laughter abound,
Your heart skips a beat to this wacky sound.
Join the funny chaos, let's travel and roam,
For in this tick-tock world, you'll feel right at home!

The Artisan's Series

In a shop made of gears, the laughter flows,
A tick-tock tickle, where folly grows.
A wobbly clock grins, so bold and bright,
Telling time wrong, what a silly sight!

With springs that bounce and pendulums dance,
Each little piece in a clumsy prance.
The cogs like clowns in a circus ring,
Jesting with time, what joy they bring!

Gears collide with a comedic clank,
While laughter's the fuel in the artisan's tank.
A timepiece jester, with a ticklish face,
Chronicles giggles at a breezy pace!

So come, dear friends, to this merry place,
Where watches in jest make the slowest race.
In a world where minutiae are absurdly grand,
The artisan's series, a funny wonderland!

Musing in Mechanics

In a workshop of whimsy, where quirkiness reigns,
The clocks tell tales of their laughable pains.
A cuckoo that sneezes, a timer that slips,
Every tick is a chuckle, oh how time trips!

With springs that chatter, and gears that giggle,
The pendulums wobble, oh how they wiggle!
A wristwatch that dances, it twirls with flair,
Just try to keep straight, you might lose a hair!

The hands on the clock seem to lose their way,
They wobble like jelly on a hot summer's day.
Each moment a jest, a delightful charade,
In this musing of mechanics, laughter won't fade!

So pause for a moment, and give it a whirl,
Let the antics of time take you for a twirl.
With each little tick and a tock that we share,
Life's a hilarity with nuts and bolts everywhere!

Whirl of the Hour

In a whirl of cogs, the fun starts to spin,
As clocks sport mustaches, and giggles begin.
They tickle the seconds, with merry delight,
A punchline in every hour, oh what a sight!

The big hand's an actor, the little hand's shy,
Together they frolic, making time fly by.
With gears that chat gossip and springs that tease,
Every chime is a jingle, a reason to please!

The pendulum swings with a jig and a jump,
An oscillating dancer with a cheeky thump.
In laughter's embrace, they rhythmically twirled,
Chasing the moments that sweetly unfurled!

So set down your worries, let the clock unwind,
Join in the fun, leave your trouble behind.
In this whirl of the hour, with laughter to claim,
Time's a goofy partner in this ticklish game!

Chasing Shadows

Chasing shadows of gears in a dappled light,
Where giggles and chuckles turn day into night.
The clock strikes a joke and the pendulum grins,
With each little tickle, the laughter begins!

A shadow in the corner, it wiggles around,
A timer that dances, it leaps off the ground.
With quartz that tickles and springs that sigh,
These giddy machines make time zoom by!

In a playful duet, the cogs come alive,
Telling silly stories where whimsy can thrive.
And shadows join in, in a clumsy ballet,
Where time is a jester, come join in the play!

So heed not the minutes, let laughter take flight,
In a world of mechanics, there's joy in each night.
For chasing the shadows brings smiles without end,
When clocks are your comrades, and laughter's the trend!

The Ballet of Springs

In a workshop, gears twirl and spin,
Springs do a dance, oh where to begin?
Tick-tock, they giggle, winding so tight,
Clock hands sway left, then winter to bite.

Cogs wear top hats, springs in ballet shoes,
They leap and they prance, sharing their views.
With a wink and a whirl, they twirl on the floor,
Time's a jester, asking for more.

The pendulum sways, a grand maestro,
Conducting a symphony all in a show.
Tick-tock bribed the cuckoo, dance on the hour,
While the clock strikes a laugh, in its final power.

When spring's gig giggles, the gears shout hooray,
In this clockmaker's realm, it's a comical play.
So give a round of applause and cheer,
For the ballet of springs, we hold so dear!

Encased in Moments

In a glass case, moments trapped tight,
Dust bunnies dance in soft candlelight.
Each tick is a laugh, each tock a delight,
Watches chortle, an odd little sight.

Marbles roll free, caught in the beat,
Their jingles and jangles, oh what a treat!
Time's busy busking, with coins in its hat,
All revelry ends when the cat comes to chat.

Pockets are loaded with seconds and minutes,
Chapter by chapter, just see how it spins.
Bottled-up laughter, these tick-tock reflections,
Catch them each week at the "Chrono Confections."

While hours do tick, moments wear smiles,
Bottled in laughter, carried with style.
So peep in that case, grab time by the toes,
And laugh at the moments, as life ebbs and flows.

Hopes Wound Tight

Wound like a yo-yo, hope's at the core,
Squeezed like a sponge, but thirsty for more.
A spring uncoils with a groan and a wheeze,
As time tiptoes by, like a light-footed tease.

Tension builds up, oh what a blunder,
It's a paradox wrapped in a moment of wonder.
Hope bounces back with a spring in its step,
As each moment tick-tocks, oh what a rep!

Like rubber bands stretched, we pull and we tease,
Winding up laughter, like bees with their bees.
The joke's in the timing, the punchline's the wait,
Hope wound real tight will soon celebrate.

So take a deep breath, let the hopes stretch high,
Flip the hourglass, let time fly and fly.
With a chuckle and bounce, let optimism rise,
In this comical twist, where humor belies.

Temporal Visions

Through time's shattered mirror, we peek and we play,
Laughing at moments that jitter and sway.
What's old is now new, and what's gone is back,
A tickle, a giggle, as time's clock goes whack!

Optical illusions hang from the walls,
With clocks looking goofy, they droop and they sprawl.
Time's a magician, in tricks it delights,
Pulling rabbits from hats on the grandest of nights.

Each tick a surprise, some wiggles, some flames,
Where days blend together, all blend into games.
Temporal visions, a carnival ride,
Twisting through laughter, oh what a glide!

So dance with the seconds, let giggles be loud,
Snapshots of time in this whimsical crowd.
For in temporal visions, we find joy and cheer,
In the merry-go-round of the moments we steer!

Imprints of Time

Tick-tock in a comical race,
Clocks are trying to pick up their pace.
Seconds giggle, minutes hop,
While hours take a playful stop.

A cuckoo with a jolly grin,
Sings to time, let the fun begin.
Winding up a merry tune,
Every tick is a laugh, a swoon.

Watch hands slipping, sliding fast,
Time is moving, but what a blast!
Each little tick is packed with glee,
Who knew time could be so free?

In the gears, the laughter spins,
Where time begins, that's where it wins.
A playful twist, a rhythmic chime,
In this clock, we dance with time.

The Dance of the Pendulum

Swinging side to side with flair,
The pendulum hops without a care.
In a waltz of seconds, watch it sway,
Who needs a partner when time's at play?

With a tickle here and a tock there,
The pendulum grins, a delightful scare.
It jiggles and wobbles, a sight to behold,
Spinning tales of mischief grand and bold.

Round and round on a lovely spree,
It drags the past into the glee.
Each swing, a chuckle, a clattering sound,
This dance of time knows no bound.

So join the fun, don't be shy,
Let's swing along 'til the stars fly by.
For in this groove, time has no fright,
Only laughter echoes through the night.

Echoes of Eternity

In the silence, a giggle rings,
Time's secrets hide, but laughter clings.
Every echo tells a silly tale,
Of tickled clocks and a humorous trail.

A whisper from the ancient years,
Brings forth chuckles, not a single tear.
"Why do we rush?" the echoes tease,
As moments dance with hasty ease.

Let's pause a second, breathe in thick air,
With time's quirks, there's joy to spare.
Forever means nothing if we scheme,
To stretch the fun, and live the dream.

In every tick, a punchline waits,
A timeless joke that never abates.
So timekeepers smile with delight,
For echoes of laughter soar through the night.

Secrets in the Ticker

Inside the clock, a party unfolds,
Where whispers of time are bravely told.
Gears are gossiping, sharing quips,
While the hands do a jig with happy flips.

Once in a while, a secret slips,
A tick that trips and a tock that flips.
"Who broke the hourglass?" they all conspire,
With laughter that spirals higher and higher!

Every tick is a bubbling joke,
Behind the face, a mischievous poke.
In the heart of the clock, life's quite sublime,
With every secret shared, they laugh at time.

So heed the sounds of clocks in your home,
Where laughter's ticking, and dreams can roam.
For within those beats, time's jesters lay,
Making each moment a bright holiday!

Mechanisms of Memory

In gears and springs, I found my past,
Tick-tock, tick-tock, memories cast.
A clock that sneezes, a watch that winks,
Time's a jester, or so it thinks.

With every tick, a story blooms,
A dance of seconds in tiny rooms.
The hour hand trips, the minute slips,
While laughter echoes in playful quips.

The pendulum swings in perfect jest,
While memories in chaos invest.
I tickle the seconds till they giggle,
As time wobbles and starts to wiggle.

In cogs and wheels, we find our cheer,
A funny thing, this passage of years.
Winding up dreams on a playful spree,
Tickled by time's absurdity!

Timekeeper's Reverie

A watch that wears a silly grin,
Tickled by hours that never begin.
With each chime, the world spins round,
While clocks do somersaults on the ground.

In a realm where minutes tease,
The days frolic with utmost ease.
Seconds chase their tails in mirth,
As laughter rings through the fabric of earth.

The timekeeper dreams in rhymes and fun,
As moments collide, like rays of sun.
Each tick a jig, each tock a dance,
In this merry world of time's romance.

Those tiny springs hold stories tight,
As hours become a playful sight.
In this reverie, we all delight,
A whimsical waltz through day and night.

The Artisan of Hours

An artisan with a crafty smile,
Whittling hours with humorous style.
Each tick crafted, a giggle sewn,
As time frolics in laughter grown.

With chisels sharp and laughter loud,
He carves seconds from a grinning cloud.
Minutes trade their suits for shorts,
As hours dance at playful resorts.

His workshop hums with joyful cheer,
While misplaced clocks spread time without fear.
"Lunch hour?" one says with a shrug,
Another misreads and has a mug!

Crafting days as if they're clay,
The artisan molds time into play.
His work, a canvas where laughter sows,
In the garden of hours, whimsy grows.

Fragments of Eternity

Fragments drift like feathers light,
In a vault where moments take flight.
Each shard a giggle, a slip of fate,
As time plays games and won't be late.

The past and future twist and twirl,
In nonsensical patterns that bend and swirl.
Seconds fall like rain from the sky,
And clocks wear mustaches, oh my, oh my!

Moments grumble and roll in their sleep,
Stirring awake in a chuckle heap.
In shards of laughter, we stitch our way,
Through fragments of time in a fanciful play.

Each jest a thread in time's grand loom,
As eternity dances in vibrant bloom.
In this merry scrapbook we keep,
Fragments of joy in our hearts run deep.

www.ingramcontent.com/pod-product-compliance
Lightning Source LLC
Chambersburg PA
CBHW070318120526
44590CB00017B/2725